THE MIND THAT RULES THE WORLD

<u>Royal Mindset Like God</u>

By

Professor Julian Businge

Royal Mindset Like God

Copyright © 2022 Prof. Julian Businge

All rights reserved. No part of this publication may be reproduced, distributed, or transmitted in any form or by any means, including photocopying, recording, or any other electronic or mechanical methods, without the prior written permission of the publisher, except in the case of brief quotations embodied in critical reviews and certain other noncommercial uses permitted by copyright law. For permission, write to the publisher at:

Greatness University Publishers
London, UK
www.greatnessuniversity.co.uk

ISBN: 978-1-913164-25-6
ISBN-13: 978-1-913164-25-6

DEDICATION

This work is devoted to each person who is on a path of developing a royal mindset; and seeks greater understanding on the kingdom of God. Now is the right time for the royal giant inside you to arise and crush the inner critic. Identity crisis is the lack of knowledge about who we truly are. Give yourself the gift of knowing and embracing your royal identity. May you enjoy royalty at its best!

ACKNOWLEDGMENTS

This book would not have been possible without the wisdom from God. All praise, honor and glory to my Lord Jesus Christ for His richest grace and mercy for the accomplishment of this book. This book has been written from the transcription of the various video recordings done on the royal civility shows in the previous years online by our royal experts under the inspiration of the Holy Spirit.

I also acknowledge the cooperation and support I have received through many individuals from the beginning of my journey as an author. First and foremost, my sincere thanks to my husband Dr. Patrick Businge for his time, support, encouragement and expertise to make this book. A great thank you to HRH King Clyde Rivers who is the royal civility Patron and also my mentor for the selfless support, training and encouragement on my journey. I wish to express my deep gratitude to my children Stella and Eric, you are my eternal treasures in my heart.

CONTENTS

Introduction 7

Kings and Priests Necessary for this World 11

What Royal Civility is All About 19

Royal Civility 29

Royal Ambassadorship and Diplomacy 39

How Royal Mindset Looks Like 53

What is Royal Mindset 61

Royal Mindset: What is it? 67

How to Discover and Develop Our Royal Mindset 77

The New and Divine Nature of God 83

Authorship Greatness 89

The Power of Your Mindset 99

What is a Royal Mindset 113

What is Royal Civility? 123

Royal Mindset Like God

INTRODUCTION

This book is explicitly created for people who want to change their lives using Biblical principles shared by experts in royalty. As you read, you will learn the secrets of the Kingdom of God. Develop strategies to improve your business. Learn ideas to create a royal mindset. Receive principles to empower yourself, and create a royal version of yourself. It does not matter where you are spiritually, physically, mentally, socially, professionally, and financially right now. You will get a life-changing mindset from this book.

As you read this book, you will discover that you are called to be a Royal Ambassador. You are called to think differently like royals. You are called to do things differently, like royals. You are called to live differently like royals. The Mind that Rules the World book is your key to living a royally defined life. Read this book and create a new world. Read this book and discover the thought patterns of God. Read this book and fulfill your royal destiny—God, class royals.

Overview of the Royal Civility Mindset Like God -
HRH Clyde Rivers

Am encouraged today because am watching the world in a crisis and what it needs is actually we got to put Christ back on top but hear this, we can't do it just from a religious perspective anymore, we can't do it from church only and what I love about this initiative is this initiative is building a culture of kings and priests.

It's important in this day and hour that we understand that we are kings and priests, there's a spiritual role and a natural role that actually we have to impact the world.

When Professor Julian Businge, our Civility Icon came up with this Initiative, I knew it was a game-changer, it was a winner, so, what I have done I have assembled the top voices in the world that I know that understand the importance of the king and the priest.

Professor Albert Nasasagare is one of the great voices in this world. He has been the special advisor to the president of Burundi, chief protocol but more than that, this man understands who God is and if I had to classify a king and priest in this earth by example, then we've to mention Professor Albert.

First of all, in the first chapter, we will be learning about why are kings and priests necessary for this world, as God's representatives here on earth, what are some of those things we need to do, how should we carry ourselves to reflect where we come from? how do you work God's work into work of the nation building process?

Royal Mindset Like God

Royal Mindset Like God

Chapter One
WHY ARE KINGS AND PRIESTS NECESSARY FOR THIS WORLD

Professor Albert Nasasagare

Kings and priests are necessary in this world because as you know the Bible said God created this world and God is the King of Kings and he managed his children to rule this world as kings. We are kings because we are prayers and praises for our most high God the King of kings so we are kings and he managed to bring his kingdom mindset to bring his identity and culture for heaven on this earth and also he call us to bring the kingdom of God in this world so that's why he managed us to be priest and king and we part of not only to implement the kingdom culture in this world but also represent heaven government in this world, we are the citizens of the kingdom of God.

1.1 Ambassadorship

Regarding God's kingdom and how we also operate. It's about the ambassadorship, we are Gods representatives here on earth making us ambassadors just like I said about kings and priests. What are some of those things we need to do, how should we carry ourselves to reflect where we come from?

The answer is simple. That ambassadorship in this modern world is a good example for who we are and our position in the kingdom of God. You know Jesus one day said the son of this world knows who we are more than the children of God, they know this is what they put for and they know this is their privilege.

For example, when here in this country the ambassador of US can misbehave but the government don't have a right to touch or to put in jail a US ambassador in this country. So, when he misbehaves in this country what we would do is to report to the US government what his ambassador is doing and his country will deal with.

So, when an ambassador is here for example in his office or home not any government in the country where he represents can do anything because that is a country he represents, no any government can enter in his residence. It will be violation with that country. So that's how we have to know who we are.

We are in this world but we are not part of this world, and as an ambassador his attitudes in behavior he tries to influence in that country to bring the culture for their embassies.

I can give you an example. For China, in every country they will build a center they will even cooperate with national university to introduce Chinese language for people to know their culture, their behavior, their belief so they try to influence, they need everybody to embrace their culture and the mentality of Chinese government is the same way with different countries.

So that's how we must act as sons and daughters of the most high God. We must be able to act because the bible says we are ambassadors of Christ, Christ was here for a short time and he did well, he finished his mission, he came to establish the kingdom of god and he set up in this country called earth to represent heaven to implement to be able to bring people in this world to be the followers of Jesus, to be members of that kingdom, that's how we have to behave in this world.

1.2 How Do You Work God's Work into Work of The Nation Building Process?

When the disciples asked Jesus how do we pray. He taught them the kind of prayer and one day he saw them they were concerned about human beings and he asked them don't think about your needs on this world but seek first the kingdom of God and other things will be added to you.

This is a powerful message, sometimes we don't think about when we are talking about that verse, you know the bible says in Jeremiah 1:4-5, before I created you I knew you before you came out of your mum I said to your part to be a prophet for the nation. It means every one of us before you exist even your parents exist; God knew you and he had a mandate about you. So, when you come into this world or when you come to leadership first of all you have to build a personal and a strong relationship with God. You bring God in everything you do; when you build a family, when you are a leader, so, that's how Burundians understood without God, we can't do anything. We decide to put God first and we know that we will be there to represent his interest and God will be involved in our leadership.

That's why the process of building our country even people they are amazed to see the progress it's not because we are special it's because we bring a special man in our everyday life, that special man is God.

1.3 How A Protocol Was Establish In Burundi To Acknowledge God

When you see the new constitution Burundi had because we had the transition concession but 2018 we had a new constitution and that new constitution is now the Burundi put God first in everything so we knew like Moses you know when God was angry with the Israeli people and he said Moses go, I will give you the angel to take you to the promised land and they must say to God we know that we are not able alone if you don't go with us we can't leave here because we know we are not able to do anything and here Burundi we realized that if God created this country, God has a plan for this country even before we exist so if we bring God in our business we succeed so that's how from now, Burundi in everything we put god first.

So, if you put God first, God is always first you become first. If you give first place to god, God is not there to be first he's already first so it's you so that's wisdom if you need to succeed in your life you invite God in your life, you put number one God in everything so you become number one.

1.4 How Can You Put God First?

Very Simple, you know when Jesus was on the cross at Calvary, He said it's finished, the mission of God did it he sent his son to save us and when He finished He sent us also to represent him and to tell people Jesus did everything for us, to put God number one and to understand why you are in this world, why God creates you and what is meant to you, you know you can't do any step without God, you invite Him to be number one in your life. It's very simple.

Lastly, I need to call everybody that the kingdom of

God is open for everybody, lets pull it together and the bible says faith comes by what we are hearing and what we are hearing comes from the word of God and the word of God says that what we believe in Christ so you have to confess by your mouth and believe with your heart that Jesus is the savior and then your life will change and you become part of the royal family.

Let us pray, Father in Jesus' name we are coming to you with faith, thank you for this platform, many people are hearing us touch every one of us and touch our people and visit your people.

Know that Jesus has finished his mission and everyone can come to him open his heart and confess with his mouth and repeat after me lord Jesus I'm coming to you, lord Jesus am a sinner I accept today that you came in this world to give your life to us now I open heart I receive you as my king and my savior thank you Jesus because you are touching your people you are visiting your people and let us understand that we are in this world as a kingdom citizen let us know that God you gave us a mission to represent you in this world and to fulfil your will give us strength and help us to fulfil your mission in Jesus' name we pray, Amen.

How to connect with Albert Nasasagare

You can google my name Albert Nasasagare or you can find me on Facebook and you can see through my position Burundi's president's office or you can find me on our youth organization called youth coalition in action YCA or you can phone me or my email address is nalbert.cga@gmail.com

Royal Mindset Like God

Chapter Two

WHAT ROYALTY IS ALL ABOUT

Pastor Michele Cohen

I think since from the beginning it's been very clear in the book of Genesis that we here to rule and that's a very royal word if you look at the meaning of that word rule in God's image and likeness, we are made in the image of the King of kings and we have the mind of Christ so we can access this royal wisdom, this higher wisdom who has known the mind of the lord that He may instruct him or understand him.

Corinthians says yet it goes on to say but we have the mind of Christ so through what Christ has done for us redemption that brings us into our completeness and our wholeness in Christ we can access that mind of Christ that's God's will for us to access his royal king of king's mind and bring His understanding, His ingenuity, solutions to the world just like any true world leader would do for the benefit of the people and that's going to be in authority, that's going to be with strength with an understanding of our sovereignty in Christ and I believe it's time for the people of God to take up this sovereignty in Christ to realize that we're seated with Christ in heavenly places.

Blessed with every spiritual blessing in heavenly realms, that we are far above all principalities and powers, all chieftains, all originations of anything that is not interested in bringing the kingdom of God and to begin to operate with that mindset of the kings of kings to bring the kingdom on earth and I think of the words of Jesus in the parable it's my Fathers good pleasure to give you the kingdom because we are co-heirs with Christ of this kingdom we've been called to rule not in our own cray ways but in his image and likeness and that's going to be the wisdom that's from above pure and peaceable full of good fruits, full of mercy and if we begin to that happening if we begin to see people really pulling out their royal robes of righteousness, we are the righteousness of god in Christ and just really activating that kind of clarity of personhood on the earth, we won't need to go down rabbit trails that lead us to stray from our true identity.

1.1 The Difference Between A Religious Mindset And A Royal Mindset

I think a religious mindset puts God in a box it's already got a plan it's got a set of rules and it's not open to what's new to what's relevant now to truly help people in their need it's more concerned with maintaining its institutional presentation that it is in helping people in need.

I think about Jesus came into a religious environment and He bypassed all of that because He was concerned with helping people He was concerned with seeing what were the needs right here right now and how can I call people into their made in the image of God identity, how can I elevate people not how can I keep people in my box for the purpose of control and I think that's a big difference. I think also a religious mindset has for too long tended in some unfortunate cases to offer a worm mentality preventing people from activating their own potential solutions to the kingdom that is at hand and so to me is huge importance between a royal mindset and a kingdom mindset wants to call peasants kings, wants to elevate people to a higher place.

The religious mindset tends to want to keep everything just so for the purpose of knowing we've got it all together and we don't want to rock the boat, Jesus loves to rock the boat because he wants to call people into an elevated place, he wants people to get in touch with who they really are and there are no limitations with God.

There are no limitations with God and so we've got to blow open the box we've got to get the lid off so that we can access the right now solutions and you see people who are maybe not openly following Christ and they're not afraid of the unlimited. That's the right power of God and so of all the people that should be truly accessing the limitless potential and power, it should be the people of God, the people who follow Christ.

I think a royal mindset is a mindset of abundance,

it's a mindset of health and not brokenness and I would even go as far as to say a royal mindset is a mindset of health and not healing. We've been getting a little bit of healing, you have to come into our health and it starts with soul health, it starts with really knowing who we are from the inside out so that we can manifest health and prosperity in all things.

It's a mindset of empowerment and not inadequacy and it knows and receives from the source, the unlimited source of all and I just love it because you know I think about how Jesus freely you've received, freely give and I believe that is a religious mindset kind of tends to not really get that because it doesn't operate in the completeness that it is established for us and so it might seem humble to have a worm mentality but it's really kind of a false humility because truly humility knows that it has nothing to do with the righteousness from Christ, it's the birthright you can't help yourself, you didn't do anything to earn that, you were born into your righteousness, payment to the awareness of your righteousness of God in Christ's position and I believe a religious mindset has not freely received and therefore it cannot freely give when we receive that absolute humility of I surrender I can't do this but I'm going to receive who you say I am God then out of that completeness in Christ we can freely give, we are just an overflowing vessel and that's beautiful.

1.2 How Pastor Michele Cohen Discovered Your Royalty

Am going to try and be very succinct I had an encounter where I came to know Jesus 31 years ago and it was powerful. Life changing and about five years after that I began to work in the ministry and I have had the opportunity of sharing the gospel message as I had learned and received it all over the world and of course I have had a beautiful 31 years.

But I will say this I brought and here is what I think is something that we can really work on as the church, as those who share the good news message is that, because the first thing I didn't hear about my made in thc likeness and image of God identity, I didn't hear about my origin, I really was continuing to hear a sort of patched up on an old wine skin story about how everything was better now from genesis 3, the departure from the garden what I needed to hear and what I think everybody wants to hear is that when you come into an awareness of who you are in Christ you bypass everything and you come back to your original identity in essence and in purpose and in everything that you are is all born of God us become in God's image and likeness and this is what Jesus did.

He would go and you would notice, this is before He went to the cross and He would address people son, daughter and I believe that healing was a natural manifestation of the realization of the identity that suddenly sprung up in people's awareness and their understanding, they were being called son, daughter, they were getting recognition in that moment of who they really are and as a result of that there really wasn't outward inside healing to be done.

It all manifests from the inside out so about eight or seven years ago I began to really ask some really difficult questions such as you mentioned if after 2000 years of Christianity was still not seeing the works of Jesus Christ being done and certainly not the greater works in general on a worldwide scale what is wrong with this picture why are so many people who proclaim a walk with God depressed why are so many committing suicide why are so many people feeling broken and in despair and are hurting and I really wanted to ask those big questions and I knew it wasn't going to be just like an overnight solution but the Lord told me to go back to the original origin of your spirit and then began to show me that in my own walk with God I had a born again experience, I had made Jesus my lord but there was a blockage in me and it was because I had brought my family origin stuff into my relationship with God.

In other words, my performance mentality, my deep-rooted sense of am not wanted. My longing to belong to all these things made me overwork, try to do something, and catch that carrot not realizing that wait a minute stop everything, it's all done and if am redeemed what am I redeemed to, that's the question because why is it we are still living like an old garment with patches and I realized I had to just let everything go and clothe myself with the mind of Christ that I really was everything that which means I'm royal, I'm still in the image of God and standing in that identity and the more I stand in it, the more I think in my heart so am I, the happier I am, the more confident I am, the more sense of purpose that I wake with every single day.

Is it a process, yes but is it a changed life dramatically so for these last seven years more so than all the 30 years behind that because of that recognition of who I am in Christ not who am going to be one day, not who am working to be one day towards but who I am in Christ.

Lastly, I want to encourage you to take a moment just to clear the slate know that God is not just our sovereign King but our Father and is so wanting us to feel safe and well and right and clear in His presence so just take a moment to do that.

Father, we thank you so much that you are so delighted to forgive us for all our sins, that Christ is our all in all that we are in Him and there is no condemnation for those who are in Christ Jesus and today right here, right this moment can be a brand new moment to step out of our peasant clothes into our royal attire to be who we are in you, born of you in your image and likeness, it's not something that we are attaining it's something that's already done and we are laying hold right now of what is already accomplished for us in Christ and we thank you that we can now take that stand with confidence and today is a new day and we are that new creature born again in our awareness of who we are as your sons and daughters, Amen.

How To Connect With Pastor Michele Cohen

trophylakes.org is the church where am an associate pastor, and also michellefrancesca.com is where you can see my blogs. Really, we operating live from Facebook right now and enjoying a wonderful live program every week with some amazing guests including of course Clyde Rivers and you can pick up on those. So, find me at Michelle Francesca Cohen is my Facebook timeline name. Thank you so much.

Royal Mindset Like God

Royal Mindset Like God

Chapter Three
ROYAL CIVILITY

Dr. Will Moreland

When I think about royalty and I was so intrigued by your topic and by this discussion. I think it's such a needed topic for where the world is right now and especially for those of us who profess to be Christians, I think it's so important for us to identify with our royalty. You know the bible says we are in this world but we are not of this world.

It reminds me I've had the opportunity to live in five different countries and as I would travel to these countries and in these countries I would always identify where the U.S Consulate was no matter where I'm in the world and if you understand about a consulate, you understand that that consulate represents a government in a foreign land so when you would step into that continent even though you were in a different country and you stood in the consulate you were in America when I stepped in that consulate I had privileges of an American citizen and so when I think about royalty and the kingdom of God when you step into your royalty and when you step into the kingdom of God, Jesus said when you pray let it be in heaven as it is in earth so that means you should be experiencing the same thing that heaven is experiencing so whenever you feel as though heaven is experiencing it you should be experiencing it here on earth and so as kingdom citizens no matter where you are in the world when you step inside the kingdom, there's another word I want to introduce it's called diplomatic immunity.

When I travel, I live now in St. Martin but I have

diplomatic immunity that means there are things that this government even though am in their country that can't do to me and it is the same thing we as believers when we tap into our faith and our royal civility. The Bible says no weapon formed against me shall prosper because we have spiritual diplomatic immunity.

1.1 As Kingdom Citizens, What Are Some Of Our Legal Rights

Your first legal right I think all of us should understand is even goes beyond legalities, it goes to heritage, the Bible says we are joint heirs with Christ so even beyond legalities we have a heritage in Christ so what does that mean.

It means Jesus is not only my savior but He happens to be my brother, it means that God is not only sovereign God but that means He's my father and when you look at the life of Jesus and the boldness of Jesus, He walked in that authority, He would commonly tell the authorities you can't do anything to me that my father doesn't allow you to do to me and so when we start tapping into our legal state as a son of God as a reward of the kingdom. You begin to understand am reminded of the parable of the prodigal son, he said you know what the servants in my father's house are living better than me, the bible literally says when he came to his right mind, many believers are not living in the authority that's available to them because they're not in their right mind. This is why the bible says you must be renewed in your mind daily because before you became a kingdom citizen, you were living according to this world and so now you need to have your mind renewed to realize you are now royalty.

You are a part of royal priesthood and so when you start talking Dr. Julian about the legality part of it some of the things that are our benefits you have access, that is the number one benefit of a kingdom citizen you have access to the King. This is why the Bible says come to the throne of grace boldly that means am not walking with my head down it's not walking like I'm some sheepish servant even though I serve I walk to the throne of Grace because who's sitting at that throne is not just a king, it's my father and now I realize and I respect him as the sovereign but I have a different relationship with him. He's not only the sovereign, He's my father and you know when you look at the queen where you are, she's the queen but to her children she's their mother so they understand proper protocol, they understand who their mother is but at the same time that's their mother and access is totally different for a child of the king than it is for anybody else.

1.2 How "Dr. Will Moreland" Walked Into His Royal Life

I was raised in the church by my grandmother but I always like to say I was religious and not kingdom so every Sunday, Wednesday night we would go to service and I would remember everything that the pastor would say offer repetition. You know the Bible says thy word have I hid in my heart that I would not sin against him well I would remember scriptures simply because I heard them a hundred times.

The word wasn't a part of me the Bible says the word must become flesh and then dwelt amongst men, well I heard these scriptures but my problem Dr. Julian was I said okay, I know that my grandmother, I know she loves God, I know these people love God but their lives were not reflective of royalty and when I was around 20yrs old I began to question God and I said God if everything in your word is true, you want us to be the head, not the tail, you want us to be above only and not beneath, you want us to be blessed going and blessed coming out, why isn't this reflective in your people, why am I not seeing this, why are they not living this abundant life, why are they not living of this dominion and I was genuinely asking him and I believe God my father heard my heart cry that I wasn't questioning him but I wanted to know if am royalty if am royal priesthood why was I struggling, why was life so hard for us.

And then God began to tell me He says your life is going to be a reflection of your faith, your life no matter how much you love me, no matter how much you come to church your life is going to be a reflection of your faith because the Bible says in Hebrews any man that comes to God must believe that He is God and that He is a rewarder of them that diligently seek them so the bible says without faith it's impossible to please God.

It doesn't matter how many times you come to church, it doesn't matter how many times you read your bible, it doesn't matter how many gospel songs you listen to he says without faith, I started studying all the scriptures on faith and I started to realize that as a Christian our whole life is centred around faith, the just shall live by faith, we walk by faith, we overcome by faith, we are the righteousness of God through faith so when I realized that the faith was the engine to this whole thing Jesus asked his disciples a question he said how is it that you have no faith so Dr. Julian it's possible that you can go to church every week and still have no faith. So, the Bible says in Romans 12, God has dealt with every man the measure of faith that when you become a believer everybody gets dealt the measure of faith because the bible says God is no respecter a person.

He doesn't give you more faith than he gives me, he gives us all an equal amount of faith then the bible says faith comes by hearing so now once God gives me that faith it's incompetent on me to build that faith. Faith comes by hearing so whatever area I want to access God in I have to start hearing his word because the Bible says he stands over his word to perform it, he doesn't stand over my emotions, he doesn't stand over my church he stands over his word and so then I realized that Gods word is his faith so once I realized that Gods word is his faith then the only thing as a believer that you should be speaking is the word of God and so as you speak the word of God, you're speaking Gods faith.

So God says let the weak say that I am strong because that's Gods point of view, God doesn't see you as weak, he sees you a strong and so what Gods trying to do he says let this mind be in you in Christ Jesus who thought it not robbery to be equal with God. Now we are about to get deep if you really want to walk in your royalty you have to see yourself as royalty He said He thought it, not robbery to be equal now equal doesn't mean saying he didn't say we are God but we are made in His image, we're made in His likeness then we are equal and God showed us in Genesis how He handles things.

The bible says when the earth was without form and void. God said let there be light, he never addressed the darkness, he only talked about what he wanted to see so as believers you can only talk about what you want to see. You can't talk about what you have and you can't talk about what you don't have, you can only talk about what you want to see and so as a believer what I see is what God sees, am the head and not the tail, am above only and not beneath.

Though I walk in the shadow of the valley of death I will fear no evil because for thou art with me how can you lack if he's with you.

See I have two children and the way I provide for them is out of my heart, it's not out of their resources, it's not out of their understanding. Sometimes I go to the store with y 10year old son and he wants something and he will look at the price and he will say Dad that costs too much and I'll say it's not predicated on what you can afford, it predicated on what your father can afford and if it's not too much for me son, it's not too much for you and so he's being blessed by his father's ability and this is why the bible says God has cattle on a thousand heels and so when you tap into faith Dr. Julian, faith changes everything.

1.3 The Difference Between A Religious Mindset And A Royal Mindset?

When you're religious you just doing things out of habit, I went to church for years out of habit because that's what I did on Sunday. I didn't go there to develop the relationship with my Father I just went there out of habit when I finally got into a relationship with him I fell in love with learning about Him, I wanted to know more about Him and so when a person just has a religious mindset, religious attitude they are only just thinking about particular things that they do but when you are in a relationship now you are really talking about how can I make this relationship blossom, what can I do for you and so when I think about having a kingdom royal mindset it's how I can advance the kingdom not how can I advance myself but how can I advance the kingdom because I realized if I advance the kingdom am advancing myself because I am the kingdom.

Lastly, Father we thank you for every listener that we've been able to use this platform to share your word, your life-changing word now my prayer is that for every speaker that has spoken that their words penetrate the hearts of every listener and that that listeners life is transformed and as they are transformed farther they begin to walk out in the trueness of life what it means to be a kingdom and a royal citizen that they would let their light shine that men may see your good works and glorify the father, father we thank you've done thus far and everything that you're going to continuously do continue to smile upon us father as we as your humble servants walk this earth as members of the kingdom in Jesus' name we pray, Amen.

You can simply follow me on any social media @drwillspeaks, am on all social media platforms.

Royal Mindset Like God

Chapter Four

ROYAL AMBASSADORSHIP AND DIPLOMACY

Dr. Alicia M Liverpool

As God has redeemed us, he also esteemed us as Kings and Priests and we will find that in Revelations 5:9-10. It is something that over the years I have noticed that not much emphasis is placed on our identity in Christ. He not only redeemed us, the Bible says He redeemed us to God and has made us kings and priests so as surely as we believe we are redeemed as surely, he has esteemed us. So, we are redeemed and we are esteemed and that is the proper balance that I bring to the teachings that God has given to me. And that truth has to permeate everything that you do, so as royalty not only is that our identity to walk with God, it is also what is necessary to get us to fulfil our destiny because it's our legal identity in Christ and He is the King of kings –who are the kings that he is king of. Well he is our king so that understating is what brings us to the rule as Priests and our rule as Kings. So, we have a role and responsibility as priests to minister and then we have the rule as Kings.

1.1 The Royal Generosity

If we look in the book of 1st Kings 10, when the Queen of Sheba came to Solomon the Bible tells u and I quote this because I believe in this so much. It says "Now King Solomon gave the Queen of Sheba all she desired, whatever she asked besides what Solomon had given her according to Royal generosity". He gave the Queen of Sheba according to the royal generosity, so it's written. Then we read in Esther where the King gave gifts according to the generosity of a king. One of the ways you can distinguish a king is their ability to be generous. They are generous with their time, generous with their help, their finances. According to the word of God, one of the ways we can identify a king is by their royal generosity. A true king is not cheap, they give gifts according to the generosity of a king and that comes from their generous heart because think of it Professor Businge, the God or the King we serve or that we emanate from because we are ambassadors of Christ for Christ is generous with us, he does not deprive us of anything that is beneficial for us, he daily loads us with benefits, that's generosity.

He supplies us with whatever we need, all we have ever needed His hand provides, He is a generous King and if we are representing a generous King then in accordance with His generosity, we also must be generous. Now it doesn't mean that we do it ill-advised or unadvised but I believe that the spirit of God in us has to be representative of the king that we said we serve.

Generosity is one of the principles for every Royal. It distinguishes a King, one who is called to walk in this royalty. It distinguishes us, it's one of the marks of distinction.

1.2 The Royal Conduct And Behavior

When we look at the book of 1st Samuel 10:25 and it says that "Samuel explained to the people the behavior of Royalty" there was a certain department of royalty, there is a certain way that royalty carries itself. It's not an arrogant behavior, its confidence in who God has called you to be.

When a king is faced with great trials, encountering situations, Kings behave in a manner that is consistent with who they are. Royal behavior cannot be overlooked, cannot be under estimated. You never hear of a King speaking luck, wondering how he is going to pay his bills, you never hear our king cursing out other people.

So then how is it that we will easily say am a daughter of the king, child of the king -that is true. We cannot refute or debate that but what we can debate is the fruit that you exhibit that is inconsistent with what you say you are and whose you are.

And this even goes deeper how you carry yourself, are you an exemplary example in your workplace, in your marriage, in your parenting, anywhere God put you? That bringing that royal mindset, because that's where it begins. The issues here is not in our abilities per say but in our mentalities.

Do we mentally agree with God, do we have the mind of Christ when it comes to understanding who he has made us to be and that is where if it's not in our spirit and flowing from our heart then there will be inconsistencies all the time.

But when I know whose I am and who I am in God that affects the way and influences every decision that I make. I am not going to be worried as a daughter of the King, the Bible tells me "the birds of the air toil not, neither do they speak yet your heavenly father looks after them, then he says are you not of more value than them.

So, if the birds don't worry where they getting their next meal from, how then as a king am, I concerned to the point of worrying how I will be fed. The Bible says "seek he first the Kingdom of God and his righteousness and all things shall be added" so when I think like that am thinking in a manner consistent with what the word of God by constitution.

The word of God is the constitution of the kingdom. My constitution constitutes how I live, how I think, how I behave. So, in accordance with the constitution, the constitution tells me don't worry, so as a King I have to elevate my thoughts that I am not going to ascend into worry, am going to ascend into worship. I have a choice and so the purpose of trainings like this is to cultivate in you the behavior that is consistent with who you are and whose you are.

Some of the ways of conducting yourself in royalty is meekness. The Bible says "God resists the proud, but that gives grace to the humble". Even though we know we are royalty God has given us power we have the king, we are dawned with so much power, we carry so much grace and angels are watching over us, we must walk in humility and that is why I like Royal Civility. Our backbone is knowing that everybody is somebody, nobody is a nobody. We see the best in everyone because everybody is a representation of God himself, he has created everybody in his own image.

These are the type of things that we need more in the kingdom because every time you hear it, it reinforces who you are and understanding. The Bible says "if any man thinks of himself to be something and he is nothing, he deceives himself" - Revelations. Well we are not deceiving ourselves we are royals by blood, by the blood of Christ.

He redeemed us and He esteemed us to share in His royalty and I can't think of any other blessing that gives me grace and peace and excitement to know that in this lifetime someone thought me worthy enough to become royalty. It's such a honor and it's a honor of royalty.

So, where we understand that this is conferred on us the Bible says "it's not by works lest any man should boast" so the only boast thing we do is our boast is in the lord. We brag on our father being a King and he has given us access to share in his Kingship and that is amazing.

1.3 God Has Given Us The Keys to Unlock, To Speak, To Co-Create

People are destroyed for a lack of knowledge; we are not living consistently or to the standard. Let me back pedal a bit –what royalty really means He redeemed us and esteemed us it is to the standard of Christ and the stature.

So, we are looking at the standard and royalty in title doesn't mean anything if we are not functioning as royalty in standard and in stature according to his word. So, if we look at Ephesians 4, here is what it says "till we all come to the unity of the faith to a perfect man to the measure of the stature of the fullness of Christ".

That is what the Royal Civility institute is all about, developing persons, it is training for reigning so the measure that God wants us to attain is fullness. We may be walking right now in a measure of our royalty but God doesn't want us to remain at the measure, he wants the measure to be the fullness in

Christ. So royalty is not just about having a title, that's not what Christ intended, He intended that we come into the fullness of Christ according to the standard and stature. In the book of Luke 1 or 2 we read that the child grew in wisdom and in stature and in favor with God.

It is talking about Jesus, so if this is Jesus and he had to grow into this, how do we proceed and think we can come into the fullness of Christ without having the goal. We are pressing towards the fullness, so when we look at our lives there is something called the language of kings, the stature of kings, the generosity of kings, the royal behavior of kings, the royal priesthood, the royal robes. By king we understand that I am king because I can rule myself, we have to succeed the first level of ruler ship for us is on a personal level.

A personal dimension of ruler ship and peace must be experienced in us before we can express that dimension publicly. So, if we do not succeed in governing ourselves then how can we succeed in governing the outer forces of our lives.

Esther understood this principle, in the book of Esther 4 the word of God tells us that both Esther and Mordecai understood that Haman had a plan to annihilate the Jews.

The Bible shows us the distinction of royalty, we can be faced in life with identical situations, identical problems and we each handle it differently why because it depends on our level of consciousness, the mind of Christ, and the royal mindset that we bring to situations. The bible says that Mordecai put on sackcloth and ashes and began weeping and wailing with aloud and bitter cry.

The Bible says that Esther heard what was happening, she sent garments to Mordecai to change his garments but he refused. The Bible says Esther, in Chapter 5 verse 1, says she changed her garments and put on her royal robes and she stood in the entrance facing the king.

1.4 The Royal Robes

Am delighted to do this because it has changed my life when I understood this truth, I have a choice in every matter that am faced with in my lifetime on this earth. I can choose when I hear of a betrayal, when I hear of someone who wants to annihilate, when something drastic happens, when something painful happens –I have a choice.

Mordecai put on sackcloth and ashes, Esther in the identical situation put on her royal robes and she didn't say a word. She stood before the King and got his attention, he extended the scepter to he, she drew close, and touched the scepter and she was able in a series of events to save her people. When we are faced with difficulties what are we putting on – sackcloth and ashes or are we putting on our royal robes. Because here is what the word of God tells us to do which is so important to realize, it says, which brings me into protocol and diplomacy, in Esther chapter 4 that "no one clothed in sackcloth and ashes may come before the King" so even though Mordecai legitimately was worried for his people, he was distressed.

The Bible says he was deeply depressed and so was Esther but even being deeply distressed, we are not absolved from our responsibilities. To save our world will not require us every time we see something on TV, every time there is pandemic, every time there is an issue in the world to put on our sackcloth and ashes and be crying, weeping and wailing, we need to put on our royal garments and go before the King and plead on behalf of nations, to plead on behalf of our people.

We have been called to the kingdom for such a time as this, it is not for us to see what's happening in the world and descend in weeping and wailing with loud and bitter cries, It is time for us to pin our head up, put on our royal crown, straighten our crown, put on our royal robes and go before the king with a mandate. Esther was able to save millions from genocide, she was able to save her people and we can do the same, we have the same power. The same God of Esther, is the same God of Alicia, same God of Professor Businge and He does not change because He is the same yesterday, today and forever.

So, if we do it according to protocol, protocol simply means the prescribed way, the bible says "no one may come before the king clothed with sackcloth and ashes, so Mordecai even though he was weeping and wailing, he was violating protocol. There was a breach in protocol and he was hoping that in violating protocol he could still come before the king, well the king was probably hearing Mordecai weeping and wailing, and the bible says many joined Mordecai because misery loves company.

When we weep and we wail, the hurt that we are feeling is not sufficient for us to feel by ourselves we invite everybody to weep and wail with us but protocol dictates that in Psalms 100 "Come before his presence with singing, enter His gates with thanksgiving, enter His courts with praise, be thankful to Him and bless His name. There is protocol in the kingdom so you come observing protocol.

1.4 What is Royal Protocol?

Protocol is the system of international courtesy in international relations and communications. In the Kingdom of God, protocol is the prescribed way. God has to teach us because the Bible says "as for God, His way is perfect" in Psalm 18:30. I did a teaching on this last night with my group, I said Proverbs 14 says "there is a way that seems right onto man but the end of it is the way of death".

So, it seems right to us but it is not right and this is where we must confer, consult, humble ourselves and say God your way is perfect. This is why the book of proverbs tells us in all your ways acknowledge Him and he shall direct your path, what happens to us many times, we are leaning to our own understanding, that is what is happening in the kingdom. In all your ways, acknowledge Him and He will direct your path that simply means he will not lead you in a path that is inconsistent with H path, inconsistent with his will, this is why we must acknowledge him.

We must say God the way am approaching this, what is the way to approach this situation because God wants you to come out victorious and I prophesy this, God wants you to come out without injury, God doesn't want causalities in his kingdom, he doesn't want injuries in his kingdom.

You can go through a storm so we can go through situations, it doesn't mean because you are royalty that you are exempted from facing circumstances and situations, it means that you are guaranteed to come out the victorious one, to come out as the victor and not as the victim.

I would like to encourage anyone reading this book presently and those who will read it. We have logged off that regardless of the opposition that you face in this life, you are here according to Revelations to reign on this earth and whatever will prevent you and hinder your reign on this earth, we are here to help you get past, rise above, go beyond, surpass every obstacle to get your reign on this earth from a thought to a reality.

About Dr Alicia M. LIVERPOOL

Dr Alicia M. Liverpool began her ministerial career in spiritual leadership in June 2002 and has been at the forefront of advancing her unique dual mandate of Worship and Kingship—the worship of the King, and the kingship of His people ever since.

Her ministerial portfolio over the years has included the ordained positions of Minister of Worship (2003), pastoral leadership and apostolic governance to Total Praise Ministries (2006-2010), and The David Company (2010-

2018). From 2018 to 2021, to her benefit and advancement in the critical value of governance and ambassadorship, Alicia secured credentials through various courses and diplomatic studies with the United Nations Institute for Training and Research (UNITAR), the Diplomatic Academy of the Caribbean, and the IEP Ambassador Program for peace ambassadors.

A gift to humanity and beloved leader, Alicia is the recipient of several awards and honors for her work as a visionary in the sphere of spiritual and socially responsible leadership. In 2008, she was awarded the Honorary Doctorate of Divinity (DDiv) from Grace Hill Bible College (USA), and in 2016, the award and recognition as a Leader-Worth-Following.

In her current role leading the REIGN Global community, her focus is on the primacy of the spiritual and ethical values of the church in relation to our sustainable reign on this earth.

Connect with Alicia M. Liverpool at
www.reign.global

Royal Mindset Like God

Chapter Five
HOW ROYAL MINDSET LOOKS LIKE

Dr S. Regina Pierre Robertson

It is important to understand where you are coming from, who you are, who's you and what your purpose is to be who you are and I believe that in order to understand who you are and really embrace a royal mindset you have to know about the kingdom and the king. How does he think, how he spoke and continued to speak and you as a royal coming from his kingdom knowing he is the king and you are also king and priest then it's important for you to begin to look at how you are speaking?

Indeed, your words create your atmosphere. It creates for you what you are expecting. You know how people talk about laws of attraction? Well, I heard someone say recently we ought to be looking at the laws of sovcreign attraction because we serve a sovereign king and how does this sovereignty think.

If I'm to emulate him and am to represent him then surely I must look at the way that I behave, I cannot be one thing in public and something else so I behave differently when people are not around because am going to slip up I won't always remember where I am and how to behave. But if I use His language, if I adapt his mindset because he has given us the mind of Christ. So, if I have a sound mind and I have the mind of Christ then we have to stop now and begin to come here, do a comparison the way I think, does it line up to what the king says, does it line up to what's written, am I functioning myself for the kingdom according to how he designed me and he created me?

So we really have to begin to take an introspective look at ourselves, how we behave, how we speak because we are co-creators with the king. With me if I want positive things to happen for me and in my life I can't be criticizing everything complaining with everything and then my narrative then doesn't match what it is I'm expecting from team or doesn't match the behaviour of a king and a priest so the royal mindset we really have to work towards getting that in order so that we can move forward to being the kings and priests that we are created to be.

1.1 How To Feel, Do And Be As God Has Called You

I see that there's the need to make a shift to pivot from where you are to where you ought to be because for many of us including myself you, we didn't grow up in church. For instance, I got saved after I had all of my kids and when I came into life in the Pentecostal church moving from Catholicism to being an independent concept that was like the shift for me, I had to learn things that no one taught me.

Before that I never thought of before that I didn't know anything about the holy spirit and being filled with the holy spirit, all those things were new to me but one thing that I come to understand that way back in the determinate council of God before that God had a design plan for our lives and this is why He encourages us, He admonishes us not to be worried or concerned about anything because He already has the answers prepared. So, knowing that He had all the answers prepared he was going to be shifting and moulding me leading me into a process to get to where I am today.

Where I am today, I understand things I didn't know before that was already in me. It was already in my DNA with my RNA in my gnome because I have the gnome of God, all the cell structures the same I am constructed and manufactured like Him so it's all there and ready for me to move on it, believe Him and work on it and so having said this, I had now to go to, that was an invitation from God to go to Romans 12:2 and what I had to do now was to hear the word of God, what He said in Romans 12:2 and then he had to take me now because he wants to transform me.

We have to get to a place of transformation and we have to be willing because he will not Drag you, you have to be willing. You have to have the desire so with that desire He took me from Romans 12 back to Genesis 1:26 to 28 to let me know that with the desire He has given me dominion and authority.

I now have the dominion and authority that was given to me, so I can now with that mindset with that authority He's given me the power to be and become, He's given me the power to make changes based on my desire and understanding of who I am. I do love to research I see a word I go and I'm looking for that word and what that word means how do I see myself in that word and based on what I'm learning from that word, I realized the changes that I have to make in me because everything that the power, the authority, the dominion to be and become has already been given to me.

But I just have to have the desire now to apprehend it and begin to see myself as how he sees me and that's how I work on me and I encourage others to work on themselves because you have to believe Genesis 1:26-28. The dominion you've been given, the authority you've been given and the power that comes with the authority and to know that He says occupy until I come.

No man can't stop you, no man can tell you who you are and can tell you what you can and cannot do because you've already been told who you are and the power that lies behind and within who you are as a royal, that's how I see.

I just want to encourage you today to realize that

everything that you are, everything that you want to be is already there. It's already in there and what you have to do is to have the desire to become who you were created to be and to just focus on becoming.

you know Michelle Obama wrote the book Becoming Michelle Obama but people focused on the word becoming ,just focus on becoming who God said that you are and to know that as your king and you are his subject everything that you need is already taken care of amen.

I'm going to go with that today I'm going to hook that today and run with that, everything that I need has already been provided and taken care of.

About Dr S. Regina Pierre Robertson

Dr. S. Regina Pierre Robertson is an Ordained Apostle, Mental Health Professional, Leadership/Retreat Consultant, Stress Management/Life Purpose Coach, Author, Transformational Speaker, Educator, Entrepreneur, and Program/Conference Developer.

She is the Founder and President of New Dimensions Global Fellowship, Inc. Ft. Lauderdale FL, an ecclesiastical and outreach model developed to address the need for purpose-driven care from the pulpit to the pew; she is the Visionary and Co-Creator of New Dimensions Global: A Faith-Based Community Mental Health Initiative that is designed and inspired with a moral imperative to go beyond current world systems, doing no harm, but moving with a quest that is intentional and significant to initiate transformative change within the Global Village; and the Global Leadership Mental Health Summit which was successfully launched on WHO: World Mental Health Day 2020 as a Virtual Forum in accordance with the United Nations #3 Sustainable Development Goal 2030.

Royal Mindset Like God

CHAPTER SIX

WHAT IS A ROYAL MINDSET

Dr. Betty Speaks

One may think royalty when they hear prince this or queen that but it actually begins within us, we can have a reflection of royalty right here in our own heart, the way we walk, the way we carry ourselves, who we accept in and out of our lives that's where royalty begins. It begins in our mindset; we don't have to let another person based on their finances or what they have inherited allow them to be of royalty.

1.1 What Happened When David Met Abigail

You know Abigail put up so much with her husband and us as women we can put up as so much from our husbands, our children, our parents we can go on and on but if you endure and constantly praying, am telling you Abigail went through much with her husband and when he died, David said am going to take Abigail to be one of my wives because she is a woman of status, I don't want to allow her to become a concubine.

So, in our life if we continue to press on, if we continue to endure because we already know the presence that he has within us, we just have to exhume that presence, continue to walk that walk, be faithful with who we are to Him, continue to walk in his presence and he will bless us. Abigail knew that David had all these other wives but he was protecting her because she was a woman of status in society.

1.2 About The Battle In The Mind

the battle is in the mind and the only way to overcome it is to say be modest, be poised and don't show pride in the things that you do, just be poised about the things you encounter allow that to be a reflection of who you are because when someone can see your reflection, they are going to start asking you questions, they are going to want to know how did you get into this position, how do you have people following you, why are people looking up to you.

They are noticing your reflection, you don't have to be boastful or loud or be seen, you can be invisible as my sister has said, those invisible acts are the ones that will show up for you and your life and l have to say you don't need anyone to validate who you are. Let the reflections of royalty be your validation.

About Dr. Betty Speaks

Dr. Betty Speaks is a renowned International speaker, leader, life coach, Ministry Minister, wife,and mother. This Army Retired Veteran has decided to use her voice to make a difference in the lives of not only adults but also children.

Dr. Betty Speaks is the CEO of A Life Change NOW, Host of Overcoming Battles by Being

Strong and Courageous. The Artist/Songwriter of the Single "It's A Resurrection. I am your Lifetime Royal IMPRINT EMPRESS! Shout out to my brother Donald Toldson, I am very passionate about MOTIVATING individuals to resurrect and establish themselves spiritually, personally, or professionally. I am also known to be that chosen WARRIOR who INSPIRES others to create A Life Change Now by leaving an INTENTIONAL IMPACTFUL IMPRINT for INFINITY. Dr. Betty Speaks, messages are filled with positivity and encouragement. She inspires her audience in the use of their voices to speak the truth and to stand up for what is right.

Dr. Betty Speaks, is is adored by her husband, Sidney, and the couple frequently looks back on their relationship, marveling at how God's work brought their lives together. They met in Fort Lee Virginia on an Army base and have lived a loving life.

Many other couples, family and friends have looked at their relationship with admiration, as one to reflect on and model themselves after. Through their years together, their love has stood the test of time and has been strengthened. They understand that love is a journey and want all couples to know that too.

Dr. Betty Speaks, has been asked to speak at various VA veteran locations, to share her personal story of triumph in the face of adversity. She teaches veterans how they too can re-enter the society and live a more normal life again after serving in the US military. She served for over 15 years as an army veteran, and she is now giving back to her peers (both in active duty and retired) by teaching them that they have both a place and voice in the society.

She is also passionate about speaking on behalf of the youth. She uses her public speaking skills to help give a voice to children who have been silenced or left behind. It is one of her goals to raise their awareness so that they know they have a voice and that their opinions are valid.

Through her seminars and speeches, Betty's students have understood that they have the right to speak up. The cause of helping others to find their voices is particularly close to Speaks' heart. For most of her childhood, Betty grew up feeling alone, unheard, and unloved. She came from a quiet, dark, place and remembers how helpless someone can feel when their voice is suppressed or silenced.

Rather than giving in to the darkness, she instead decided to turn to the light and give her life to God. Today, she is known as someone who gives love wherever she goes, by empowering women and men to live their very best lives.

You can find Dr. Betty Speaks most days on a platform speaking, her effervescent personality filled with energy and passion for people's movement into living lives filled up with truth and love.

She has teamed up with some amazing speakers and has traveled around the country with influential leaders like HRH Clyde River, Professor Ruben West, Robin Roberts of ABC, Lisa Nichols, Cheryl Woods, Les Brown, Willie Jolley, Andy Henriquez, Dr. Vernet A. Joseph, Laveda Whitfield and many more.

In understanding Betty's perspective of life, here is one of her greatest heart's desires. That others would agree, receive and accept what God says about them, because He knows them best and loves them enough to recognize their Royal Identity While Embracing His IMPRINT.

Stay in touch with Dr. BETTY SPEAKS

www.bettyspeaks.com
Facebook:https://www.facebook.com/betty.speaks.

CHAPTER SEVEN
ROYAL MINDSET, WHAT IS IT?

Dr. Charles Anthony

I wouldn't say it's self-explanatory but I would say it is a mindset. I think you can come from any genre, you can come from any culture, any walk of life and the way your mind is developed the way you think about yourself your purpose, the way you think about who you are not only in the world, the space you talking up but also in Christ and perceptively when we referencing Christ we referencing our DNA.

I was speaking to someone the other day and actually was talking to my wife and I was talking about how when you want to keep someone alive, let's say in the natural let me put it this way and they say they need a blood transfusion and in that transfusion they say I have to find someone with a particular blood type that you have and I bridged the gap on that and I said well when you want to stay alive in Christ when you have a royal mindset, you already have this blood type but in order to stay alive in Christ you have to embrace the fact that you already have the blood type.

You will seek out Christ and you seek our Lord and in that seeking that brings life into you and I hope am explaining this well to you because I think about what gives life. When I think about our royal mindset, all of these questions run through my mind what dictates royalty, is it what somebody says or is it a task you take on and nobody else could and when I considered this even this morning I said it's all about the way you think of you. If you don't think of yourself as someone who is raw if you don't think of yourself as someone who has a part of Christ's DNA, if you don't think of yourself as someone who is connected to all other royalties then there are some of the things we have to re-evaluate about ourselves.

Royalty only has to do with what you think of you, I believe royalty also has the influence of the people that you are around, the influence of the people who you associate with. Someone said this that everyone that you associate with witness seem to be pulling from you more and you're not getting nothing from them then you need to find another set of friends.

You need someone that is going to help you grow and become royal great and understand purpose. It's not about giving out all the time so royal mindset, is the way you think of you. It's understanding your connection, understanding your DNA, embrace who you're in Christ and I'm trying to stick with the best definition of it but I have a whole bunch of things that run through my mind about it.

I think it has a lot to do with the way you think about yourself regardless of what those around you consider you to be or what they believe about you.

1.1 Steps You Can Take To Be As God Has Called You

1st Peter 2:9 says: but you are a chosen race, of royal priesthood and a holy nation of people for his possession and that you read on and said that you may proclaim the excellences of him who called you out of darkness into his marvellous life.

I was considering you know but he said you are a chosen race and a royal priesthood so he already proclaimed what we are a holy nation, based on the authority and based on the DNA he is already ushered into our live so he already said this is what we are, this is who we are and he said the people for his own possession and we as in possession referencing his belonging.

Everything that belonged to Him, we are people that belong to him and we belong to him that means He gave us the authority to have as you all reference dominion over the things that He gave us dominion over here on earth so I was considering this and he said you proclaimed the excellences that of him who called you out of darkness and so when you're in darkness there is a deep-seeded mind-set that you have that says that I don't belong or I can't see or I can't identify or I feel like there's a void so when he called us into his marvellous light there and when we go into the light there is an identity that is exposed right there, we come from not being able to know who we are, what we are, who's we are into His marvellous light and I moved to the scripture that says see ye first the kingdom of God and everything else will be added and as I am seeking the kingdom well as I'm seeking everything that he's already given me already ushered here on earth from heaven and said we ought to reflect him in earth because obviously he said we are citizens. So, we reference the idea of colony being belonging to and so the possessions and things that he's already gave us dominion over and as we seek these things and what we are seeking when we seek the light of Christ. We're seeking power, we are seeking the authority, we are seeking the love, we are getting in a position.

I know that you all saying that I'm royalty but how do I define that royalty, what is God saying about that royalty. What is it that gives me the authority to even say I am royal? and so there's an authority has to follow and that authority is given to Christ. The bible says in Matthew 28 that all authority on earth has been given to me so he's identifying that anything I say even in new testament church anything I say comes from the Father himself.

So, if I say that you're a royal priesthood and you're a holy nation, that's what you are but being able to embrace that identity is what becomes a difficult task because societies tell us that we're no good, people tell us that we don't look good, the tasks that we're giving in life become so hard for us that we feel like some are privileged and some are not. They got handouts, we didn't, we have all the things that run through our mind that tells us that we are not worthy of what God has for us but when it talks about being able to embrace all that God has given us and we are seeking it.

I'm going to go biblical with this is God breathe so if I go to the breath of Christ and I go to the word of God and I go to the heart of the matter which is the gospel then what I'm saying is that everything I need to know is right here and if I can tune out all the other voices that is not of Christ.

That is not of the Holy Spirit speaking to me and I can embrace what the Holy Spirit is saying not only through his word but through the process of what he speaks to me as an individual.

If I can embrace this idea wholeheartedly it doesn't matter what nobody around me has to say I know how to eat the meat and spit out the bone, in other words, so being able to understand that to define my identity in the marvellous light of Christ, being able to see that my identity lies in my service to him, being able to see the identity lies when he says I'm a royal priesthood, I'm a holy nation.

Royal Mindset Like God

What does it mean when he said that I'm royal? When you think about what is a priest, what is living priestly, what is how should I dress, how should I look, how should I carry myself. Understanding the definition of what these words mean would help us get in the position to embrace that.

We have to seek what it is and when you say seek something that is telling me that it's there already, I just have to go and find out where it's. That's the way I see it so it's not like you're telling me to go look for something that's not present. God is telling me that I have this in place and I have put this inside of you so not only do you have to sit and seek for things tangibly from time to time but what I have for you, the most is deep down inside of you. We have to seek the voice of God in what you're saying to know that's what God is saying, so it's very important to seek it out.

For instance, my wife said something the other day. She said we see what God wants us to have and we see this but what the basic component is we never ask how, how do we get there, how do we love, how do we serve. You know you have to ask these questions. God tells us to do it. He says seek not to ask and so we have to follow those three components. I think to understand that we have to embrace our identity in royalty.

About Dr. Charles Anthony

Dr. Charles Anthony is a brilliant son, an incredible father and a devoted husband. Dr. Anthony is an Evangelist, motivational/ inspirational speaker, Ambassador of greatness and goodwill, Spiritual Leader, Lecturer, Teacher, Leadership expert and Mentor, Life Coach, relationship coach and Royal family expert and practitioner for Royal Civility Institute.

He has been nominated for civility humanitarian award through Greatness University and was inducted into the first of its kind "World book of Greatness 2020."

Dr. Anthony is the founder of Royalty Loyalty clothing Brand, which will be launched the summer of this year 2022. Dr. Anthony is the founder and lead Pastor of Foundation First non- denominational church located in Sidney Montana.

He is also the co-founder of H.E.R. Inspiration resource centre alongside of his beautiful wife and philanthropist Dr. Nadia Anthony who is the founder of this initiative. This is a centre that promotes pro-life and encourage woman and girls to thrive in their ability to parent and seek proper guidance that promotes life, love and spiritual inclination

Dr. Anthony is known for deep illustrations and metaphorical genres when speaking to the masses. He is known as a renowned speaker that has broken racial barriers across the United States.

His life's commitment is to educate, empower and encourage for the building of the Kingdom of God.

He has an Honorary Doctorate in Humanities from United graduate college and seminary international, recognized as a Master of Greatness from Greatness University; he has a Master's in spiritual leadership and a Bachelor's degree in biblical studies from Sunset bible institute.

Dr. Anthony has also authored the *Book of love: How to love Gods Way* and *Three pillars of a Great Spiritual Leader*. He has also co-authored books with some of the world's most renowned leaders: *Les Brown Changed Our Lives* and *Jesus Changed Our Lives*.

Dr. Anthony has demonstrated an understanding of biblical principles and has inspired and equipped teens, young adults and families to seek a deeper walk with Jesus. He has worked closely with other church leaders and administrator's business owners contributing to the task of promoting church and business growth.

Instagram: rlotaltybrand

Facebook: Royalty Loyalty

Facebook: Anthony's Bond

Chapter Eight

HOW TO DISCOVER & DEVELOP OUR ROYAL MINDSET

Professor Michal P. Pitzi

Number one we need to understand who we are and

we need to understand where we've come from and I believe that we were created in the image of a creator and we have to understand that if we were created in that image we need to understand what image that is.

In the Holy Scripture, it says we were given the mind of Christ so if we've been given a mind we should study what is that mind and what does that mind do or think and what actions come because of those thoughts and it's all over in the Holy Scripture and so you really have to understand who you are and where you've come from to understand a royal mindset and we are kings and priests then we are royalty but that doesn't mean we understand how to think, how to act and so we have to really look into if we were created in that image of a creator for example we should study that creator how he thinks and how he acts.

For example if you look in Genesis in the first chapter, we see that the Creator spoke and things appeared so if I'm created in that image the things I speak have the ability to appear so then that makes me think what am I saying every day what's coming out of my mouth and how is that creating my day. It's a very practical example of a royal mindset and what it could look like and what we need to do to get there.

1.1 Steps You Can Take To Start Developing Your Royal Mindset

Some key things have been said in the previous chapters and I'm a search at the mission so I am someone who takes it beyond theory because we hear a lot of ideas right about kingdom and kingdom mindset but if we really understood what it is to have a kingdom mindset we would see a lot more evidence and results on the earth, we'd see a lot more people not having mental health issues.

For example, so doctors literally gave a key scripture and I believe if you start with this scripture it's actually the whole, if you work on this scripture to understand it you will have them and walk in a royal mindset so we've been given a spirit of power, love and a sound mind now we've heard that before what does it actually mean so we need to understand I would say number one you need to seek to understand and what does it mean to have power as a royal and that is connected to authority if you look at a king's life, a literal king on the earth if you look at a king's life and the power that they have and the authority that they have you'll see that the king understands his or her power, that a king understands his or her authority so we need to learn to understand our authority what authority do we have I remember as a young learner I used to be afraid of so many things but I kept hearing my God is all-powerful and there's always you know I have power but I was so afraid of things so I was missing some understanding of who I was and the power that was in me even in the power of being a royal and once I understood and had the I sought to understand.

Well we have to know what we're looking for if you're just out there floating around, you're going to find all kinds of things right so we have to seek what is it, we have to understand what does it mean to have power, what is our authority as royals and then love, what does that mean, what does that look like again you just have to seek to understand what it looks like and then a sound mind, what does a sound mind look like and then once you seek to understand then you can begin to look at your own life and go wow is that being practiced in my life, do I think these things.

I say number one is to understand and to be focused on what you're seeking, what are you trying to understand or otherwise you'll be lost in the woods so if I had a piece of advice for anyone to get started on this path go study what does it mean to have authority, what do you have authority over, what does it mean to love, what does it mean to have a sound mind what does it actually look like and again I'm a practical person write it down, get it out of your mind and put it in the tangible realm because that changes things change things once you write things down it makes it tangible so I would say start with seeking to understand those three things.

With this royal mindset is we already have these things and I think tradition has misinformed us that we we're deficient, that we need to go get more that we're deficient in these areas and I believe that's a misunderstanding. We've been misinformed by tradition, we already have these things and if we look at scripture we understand that we already have these things and those are the things we need to seek to understand or else to understand or else we will believe what we've been misinformed so that's just a huge key.

We already have these things like we do not need to ask for more faith we already have it if we have the Holy Spirit, we really need to ask for him to come, things like this we've been misinformed by tradition.

About Professor Michal P. Pitzi,

Professor Michal P. Pitzi, I'm the Chancellor of United Graduate College and Seminary International. Education is my passion so I'm excited to work with the Royal Civility Institute and am also the ICN Global Educator of the year.

Royal Mindset Like God

Royal Mindset Like God

Chapter Nine

THE NEW AND DIVINE NATURE OF GOD

Dr. Sharon Anderson

I know what it means to take off that old nature and put on the new and divine nature of God so that you can be everything that God has called you to be. All things have passed away but all things have been created new. And the reason I know I was meant to come on because I wasn't going to come on and then my sister Dr. Alicia preached my trial summon and my scripture was from Philippians whatsoever things are pure, whatsoever things are lovely, whatsoever things are just, whatsoever things are virtue, whatsoever things are of good report, think on these things.

You cannot have a royal mindset if you don't change your mind, if you don't think like Christ then you can't change, and often we look at those things that happen outwardly, it all starts with you and your mindset. You have to say yes to Christ, you have to say yes to God and then you have to receive the Holy Spirit so that you can access that mindset.

The bible tells us that we have to put on the full armor of God that we have to think on these things so am incredibly grateful to be here today because this platform speaks for my testimony. I had to change the way sharing thought about sharing and I had to think about sharing the way God, my father in heaven thought about sharing.

And it was only until I received that revelation that I

was able to begin to see things change for me, the abundance, the healing, spiritual healing, physical healing, financial healing because I embraced that mindset.

1.1 Learn From The Master

Jesus got resurrection power when he went to hell and when he died on that cross. He died so that we might have everlasting life and so when we talk about royal mindset, we are saying you don't get to that royal mindset without your own crucifixion experience and when we look at what Jesus suffered, it cannot compare to any of the pain that we experience in this earthly body and so often times as we go through if you are listening on this line someone that fell into my spirit is saying not just what it is but how do I.

You all that you've overcome, well the bible says that we are overcome by the lamb and the blood of the lamb in the power of our testimony. But how do I get through this because we often times once we get there we forget what it's like to be in the process and so whoever it is that pouring on to my spirit today and saying how do I do this, I hear what you saying but am in the middle of it, you all acting look like you all got through it right and now your spirit is royal and they are calling you generals but how do I get through it? I just lost a baby, been in an abusive relationship, I just got divorced, I got an eviction notice on my paper, they've just told me I have cancer, my son is locked up, how do I turn this present pain into power.

And what we are all saying is that you have to take on the garment of the Holy Spirit, you have to take on the mindset of God and how do you do that, you have to lay down your own souls and you have to pick up that mantle that God has given to you.

You have to speak because the bible says speak those things that are not as though they are so I will not get put out of my house, I will not lose my child to the streets, I will not die of cancer, I will have the finances that I need to overcome this financial situation, the Bible says that there is power in our words so when we put on a mind of Christ that's not enough we have to speak those things and sometimes we have to speak those things to ourselves.

Someone said encourage ourselves in the Lord, the bible tells us to sing the songs of Psalm so we have to speak those things. David, when he was faced with the situation at Ziklag and they, took his children, his wife and he had nothing they thought they were going to kill him, he asked God shall I pursue and He said pursue but he had no one else to encourage him so he had to encourage himself.

So whoever is listening to that is putting on my spirit and the question that you are asking is how do I do what you are telling me to do is that through reading the Bible, through going to church, through listening to the songs, and through speaking life to yourself no matter what it looks like.

If you have to put it all over your house, post it that says I am fearfully wonderfully made and my soul knows that. You have to pick a Psalm a day to read over and over again until it goes down so that when you are on the floor wrestling because all of us have been on that floor wrestling with God just like Jacob and was left with a limp because he needed to have that experience.

So, beloved whoever it is, speak to yourselves, speak those words of encouragement and you will see that as you do that as you walk through your valley of the shadow of death that God will give you that resurrection power so that you as all of the generals can now speak to others and can bring them out of that valley. Speak to yourself that's how you do it.

About Reverend Dr. Sharon Anderson

She is an executive pastor at the Temple of Praise in Washington D.C, She is an attorney by trade, an author, a business strategist, life coach and most of all she is a humble servant of God.

Royal Mindset Like God

Royal Mindset Like God

Chapter Ten
AUTHORSHIP GREATNESS

Professor Patrick Businge

One of the things that people don't realize is systems don't change lives, it's individuals who change lives and if you have to change lives then you don't have to walk in the system and through the system, let me just give an example that's common to everyone. Look at Jesus, had he fitted into the Jewish system that he was born in, we wouldn't have Christianity or the Prophet Muhammad had he fitted into the system he was born in, we wouldn't have Islam so all these founders of religions yes they realized the system, saw the system and said there's something more to their lives than just following the system.

In other words, they are following their spiritual self and that's where spirituality comes in, you're focusing on what is authentically in you and trying to bring that out to create a better life. It's like you are following your path, less path.

You are following the path but you don't know the path but as opposed to the other side we have religion whereby everything is institutionalized, well this is how we pray, this is how we sing, this is how the religious ceremony goes on, this is what is objective, that's the truth for this group of people for this religion so you in kind of conditioned living because you aren't fit in that system, you have that system which is exclusive.

Yes we do have the truth in this kind of religion, you

don't have the truth because you're not the cause, we're based on the knowledge that this is what we know, this is what our founders heard, this is what they did, this is why they believed but on the other side one thing about spirituality and where the innovation comes from were thinking about the wisdom. So here you talked about authorship greatness, here I was thinking about the Holy Spirit educator linking us to their wisdom day by day by day to create new things, to bring things that don't exist yet.

Just to give you an example tomorrow we're having the World Greatness day celebrating for the first time, tomorrow we are doing the world induction to the world book of greatness, tomorrow we are celebrating the World Christian goodness awards that is completely new, there's no blueprint. We are doing it for the first time so if I was following this system before, I wouldn't be able to because I don't know.

Even some people asking me how do you feel about tomorrow, what's going to happen, I don't know and it will happen following the spirit as you are going to guide us. I was talking to one of the ladies see how am not sure Patrick, I don't know I haven't gotten my medals and my book what am I going to do, do I still have to and I said don't worry just follow the flow, the spirit will lead us but we are really allowing that spirit to create the path and we are following that path, pathless path.

1.1 All You Must Know About Royalty

One of the things that people need to realize here, you cannot be a royal without discovering your greatness. So greatness is a prerequisite for your royalty, what do I mean by that so there is or there are various dimensions of greatness which I could go into but may take us some time but one of the things that we fundamentally deliver in greatness is that everyone has greatness within them and that greatness originates from the creator of greatness, that great greatness originates from the greater so the creator begets greatness, the creator gives birth to greatness and that greatness is initially in each one of us, so we participate in that greatness.

So, the different components of greatness at the same time are different components of the person who created the greatness and one of those fundamental characteristics of the greater God, the creator is the royalty.

So, the creator is the overall King of all, on that kingship is shared with each and every human being that is alive, each and every human being that is great. some people realize it and go on to live their greatness, some people realize it and go live on their royalty, some people realize it and walk through their spirituality, through their authentic self-life into the kingdom of the king or the creator but some others do not, so they live lives that are not worth living.

Well because they haven't taken time to discover who they are, they haven't taken the time to discover what they want in life, haven't taken time to discover what their purpose in life is because everything has a purpose and we spend time studying about the purposes of different things but how often do we study about the purpose of ourselves.

And that's why we do our greatness, that's why we do our royal civility, we help people take a stop, look back and actually say let me study my purpose in life. There's no point of knowing that the tree can be used by 500 different uses but what about your life, is it to just go wake up and go work and that's it. So there is a missing link there, there's someone studying on in a way we would call them non-essential but we study less sick, lesser being sick in terms of purposes and the higher being which is closer related to the origin, the higher being which is created in the image of the maker is never studied as an authentic subject as a discipline and that's what we do in greatness. So, we will study great lives, we'll help people study their greatness, they develop a delivery time walk into their royalty.

1.2 Does Education Really Matters- Spirituality

You might not necessarily need higher education, yes there are people who need it but not everyone might need it, what they need is life education because life education allows you to have your own path, allows you to have your own and study your own experience and actually that reminds me a quote from the Indian author, he says religion is a belief in someone else's experience, spirituality is having your own experience.

What I'm saying in essence is that, yes, so they will say moving from the point of saying we might not necessarily need higher education but life education, why, because life education allows you to have your own path, allows you to have your own experience than following other people's experience so what do I mean by this. Before I elaborated my point I was saying that Deepak Chopra the author says religion is a belief in someone else's experience, I believe in Jesus' experience, Prophet Muhammad's experience, Buddha's experience - Buddhist but spirituality is having your own experience so my education is about finding your spiritual self and then creating your own experience.

Higher education will allow you to look at other people's experience, study those religions. I did theology at the University study other religions and other peoples experience but I was never given the chance to devote my own life experience, to reflect on my own spirituality and that's what we do at Greatness, help people get in alignment with their spiritual selves, get in alignment with their inner greatness because it's at the very core of your inner greatness.

When you're alone with yourself by yourself and with your maker, you are able to discover your gift. Once you discover your gift within you then you can outwardly manifest it. It doesn't mean that some people don't manifest their gift but for example some of those great footballers or singers you may ask them what is your gift, they might not tell you it's football or singing but say well actually I don't know because they have never reflected on that within them. Their inner self has never reflected where does all the craft they use when on the football pitch, where does all the craft I use when am holding that microphone as singing in front of a big audience come from. They don't ask that question, they don't know but for some of us think go within yourself, discover who you are and then manifest it because well you can't be great for yourselves.

You need others to show the way so you need people to mentor you, you need people to lead you to lead you on that path because the path can be lonely and then can be dark and that's why you need someone to get your cross, will hold your hand and take you to your next level.

1.3 The Different Between Religion And Royalty

Am sure there's a big difference, you can even see the difference in the wording itself, one is religion the other one is royalty. Religion from Latin is tying yourself to something and as I said earlier you are tying yourself to beliefs, you are tying yourself to institutions, you are tying yourself to something that is organized and exclusive, tying yourself to something that is knowledge based. Importantly, because its knowledge based if you don't follow the system you can't be kicked out, you can't be excommunicated so some people end up living with fear based on experience because they don't want to break the rules.

They know it's 10 commandments, follow the ten commandments and you know if you don't follow them there is punishment or judgement and so on or you have to follow the 1613 laws in the Torah but if you miss one of those according to the day then you are going to be punished but when it comes to royalty then that's different thing, why, because you are looking at the kingship, the ruler ship not of the traditional stations, we are not looking at a justice system that governs Christianity or Islam which is more invisible.

We are looking at a system that governs a kingdom and when am talking about Kingdom people may think about the United Kingdom, yes it's one of the kingdoms and you have the queen as a head and within that kingdom you have different other systems you have the political parties you have the ruling party, opposition party, different ministries and so on but I would like you to use possible similar analogy and think of a kingdom that governs the whole universe.

Religion is a tiny bit within the kingdom but it's not all because they are the spheres like politics, science, anthropology which are not necessarily components of religion but when you think about kingdom is a much bigger system that governs the whole not just the planet earth, the whole universe thinking about the visible and invisible.

1.4 Why I Established World Greatness Day?

again if you look at what's happening in the world, there are lots of people who do great things, there are lots of people who live and manifest a gift, there are lots of people who have touched other people's lives and take them and really cared for the people that helped them, empowered them but nowhere in the universal calendar I'm talking about the whole universe here, what exists we see or don't see is there a day when we celebrate those achievements.

So some people live up to 100 years, 110 and they die with their equities uncertainty can you imagine working for 100 years being alive in this planet for 100 years with greatness because I don't want people to pay that way, what do I want people to leave in this universe, I want them to at least leave a dent right in the universe of greatness.

Once you come in here with what you are holding then that's already a dent in the universe, that book will be there even when I'm dead even the people who are here when they're going 200, 300, 500 years, they will still be remembered as being great, they'll be honored, they'll be celebrated the great grandchildren they will know about them, why, because they've left a dent, they've left a dot on the universe that's why we do our greatness and on Greatness Day we celebrate their greatness through the greatness award we still pay their greatness through our inductions into the book of greatness and that I think is very important.

Royal Mindset Like God

Chapter Eleven
THE POWER OF YOUR MINDSET

HRH King Clyde Rivers

I believe you've learned a lot from the first ten chapters. Chapter eleven will be in a form of overview on what you have learned so far. I will be sharing some personal stories so that we can really understand what this book is all about and the important of our mindset.

One of the things that I think is important is that as you understand this actual book everything is predicated on the way people think. Every person that is poor thinks poor, everyone that's rich thinks rich, everyone that's sick thinks sick, everyone that's healthy thinks healthy because it's a biblical principal, as a man thinketh in his heart so is he out of the abundance of the heart this is where your life speaks and as a man thinketh.

Thinking has everything to do with where you are in life today and I promise you everywhere am at in life today is because of thoughts, thoughts that I learned how to take and how to manage those thoughts and we've created things now that are just where we are operating in the world today is above and beyond what I can ever ask or imagine so I want to say all of you in this group you are in for something spectacular because it's important that we help you learn how to walk out of the wrong mind into the right mind but hear this, this mentality has to help you win in your everyday life. We just don't want to be a bunch of people quoting scripture without the action so these things are going to help you step your game up and bring things into existence that need to be in the earth.

You know what's so important about this is it takes the right mindset to bring things into existence. Let me give you an example, six and a half years I had an idea, a thought from God for something called "I Change Nations".

I took that thought and within a six-year period, we have access to over 120 nations why you have everything to be able to bring the ideas into existence because what I believe is not by might, not by power, it's by the Holy Spirit.

What the spirit of God gives you, you have to learn the discipline to walk it into existence. Most people that I know of they don't take care of the idea long enough; they get the idea and they are off to the next.

I always tell people lots of guys if I look at you and if I can't tell what you do, you have over branded and many people that are over branded don't even try to over-brand they just get involved in actually and what they associate with brands them.

So, this is the main reason this was written. We want to help you unbrand yourself from the wrong brand

and build your brand and own that in your mind because the thoughts from God is actually currency that creates the future so when you learn how to access the currency of God, you can write the script for your future along the currency that God gave you.

1.1 Time To Use That Gift In You

You are assigned on this earth with a mission, with a purpose, you have a gift in you that you've never use because as royals we believe we are born to reign in any sphere of environment we find ourselves. In our homes we are born to reign, in our workplaces, in our businesses we must be the light, we are born to reign.

We are meant to influence, to bring change, to be the salt of the world but how do we do it, it all starts with the mind. What do you see, were do you see yourself in the next five years do you have a plan , do you have a goal, are you actually using your gifts the gift that God gave you when you came into this earth. Each one of us has gifts but do we even use those gifts.

You know what? part of that process is walking into your uniqueness. Let me share some personal experience.

When God gave me the idea for **"I Change Nations"**, no one around me understood the idea. The reality that you'll face with a God idea and with a royal mindset is God may give you an idea no one's ever had before. You have to keep your mind strong on what God said and not what they say.

That's why in the midst of the Coronavirus I prospered so much because the vision of God is not quarantined, governments may actually quarantine you but can't quarantine that that's born of God so what am I saying. I'm saying part of what you will go through as you build a new paradigm is you will go through being the only one with a new idea, that idea will not be embraced by all but as long as it is embraced by God and as you walk through those seasons. He will help you of everything you thought, you were and that's God giving you a number one mindset.

The actual work of a royal mindset, the actual preparation for it is not what other people have told you, when you follow that idea, that idea will mentor you into what you're supposed to be and create in this world because God has to mold you into what he said you'll do and be.

I had a day in my life where I wanted the biggest church in the world, I wanted to be the fastest growing ministry. Well guess what, God took that out of me, gave me the world stage and now I don't want to be on the stage He took all those things out of me and then gave me the stage and now it's my job to put others on the stage so that actual royal mindset has to hold on to the God idea and the God idea will go through times and seasons but in the end it will speak.

1.2 Benefits Of Being Around With The Right People

One of the benefits is that when you are round them you are learning, you're growing, you're expanding your capacity.

I tell people I have a word I use **ER**; everybody has **ER – "Evidence and Results"**. What I do when I look to work with people, I look at what's their ER. I stop listening to people talking and I look for what they've created because what they created is evidence and results so what you'll learn from working with us, see I have created an actual world civility culture and now this culture is operating all over the world.

I want to share with you, last year, Mama Sarah Obama the actual grandmother of Barack Obama received **"Sir Clyde Rivers disability Award created by Dr. Patrick Businge."** Now watch this here as we talked to her people, we said we'd like to offer her the first ever, they got back to us in 10 minutes and said yes why because when they googled my name, they saw the institution that's been built.

I want to encourage you, we're going to help you become number one, number one is not a person with thousand people. Number one is a person that owns the content that people can't live without. I own my content ability; I own it and it's my stage. Put this way, I do five to ten awards every month now.

I am producing so much now because when you own the stage, when you are number one you own the information that people can't live without and I'm telling you this, I don't do this stuff, I take my clients on a personal basis, I don't advertise.

I do none of this because am picky who I work with. So, I worked all over the world and I know how to make it work for you. I know how to craft you into a culture to where you are.

1.3 The Power of Faith

let's talk about faith in the kingdom for a second. Do you think what's our responsibility as believers? If you're a believer are you really using faith or do you believe? I had a guy ask me a question and he said Dr Rivers, believer is someone that believes and he says most people are stuck in faith and he says if you don't, the scripture says faith is the substance of things hoped for and the evidence of things not seen.

So if faith is substance, how do you show? I think royalty is mis-defined I think it's defined all wrong and let me kind of give you an example. I think people base royalty on the British monarchy, that's royalty and I'm going to say that is so far lower than God.

Maybe God has made us royalty as maybe royalty needs his assignment so and this is a thought maybe we look like royalty when we're functioning in the assignment he's given us.

Personally, everything I hear and step towards He does it, everything I hear and don't step towards it doesn't happen. So many times if your life feels stagnant, then check what you are not moving towards, what are you waiting for? if you're nothing shows up when you wait it, shows up when you move because this is what God gave me a vision years ago, it was some things that I had need of and the holy spirit said there's a window in heaven. Believe in God that He is able to do all things.

Sometimes God gives you the faith to hold and that thing's going to happen in five years so nothing I can do today that can make that come to pass. Because God's ordained it for five years down the road so I see many people frustrating the grace of God but what they want may not be the timing of God.

I've never been put in a position that I ever knew the word of God says when you're faithful over little and this has everything to do with the kingdom.

When you're faithful over little you become king's rule, so if people aren't faithful over little, they will never get to the ruler stage. Faithful over little means you'll rule much so basically what God is, what he does, when you understand your authority in God and your assignment and your area, you become. A principality is an actual prince over a land mass, over territories so God is looking to make us a principality over a landmass.

1.4 How Can I Grow My Royal Mindset?

What I would say at first is be obedient to what God says. You see you can't educate yourself into the mind of God, it's a revelation so people think that they can read, people think they can bring God into as if he is an academic professor, sit in a class with God and He teaches you all this stuff and then you speak it back to Him and He says an A plus now how does that really work for us.

Many people go to school get their A but they can't do the job, so with God in my opinion it's a whole another system that people don't really understand and grab at times.

God's system works off the Holy Spirit leadership of what God tells you to do so you can read the bible and miss God because the Holy Spirit is a living person so I have a relationship with a person not a book so the book is fantastic and of course the Holy Spirit will lead you to the book for certain things if you can read.

If you can't read, he's the same Holy Spirit that will lead 70% of the world that can't read. He's the same God that will lead you whether you can read or not read.

So what happens, I think we have intellectualized the spirit of God in the west and said you got to be able to how do you grow it? Its obedience, it's basically if am to walk as a believer, I'm to walk in the actual mirror of what God tells me to do. If I can hear and obey, I'll be fruitful every day of my life.

1.5 The Mind That Rules The World.

The mind that rules the world, what people don't understand is because mankind is made in the image of God, we all have the image of God so everyone has a mind of God. It is what information you allow in is the mind that rules your world so everyone's world is as big as their ideas, as big as their thoughts so except the man is born again and this is a doctrinal war man is born again when you can see the kingdom so when you see the kingdom you have the ability to produce what God wants.

So the mind that rules the world is what thoughts you let operate through your generator, through your creation center in your belly and if you meditate on the thoughts,, you get the outcome because it's a law of attraction what you think attracts to you.

1.6 Characteristics Of A Royal Mindset?

I think there's a principle that has to be followed, when you're faithful over little God makes you ruler so I do believe that everybody has royal capacities but everyone's not a ruler. The actual process is He says when you're faithful over little because as you are faithful over little that's when your faith is getting beat up that's when you're in the game and all of your ideas of who God is don't work, am just being real candid.

You two people agree and it doesn't happen, I mean you're believing God for something and it doesn't happen and as you stay in there then God gives you what He wants and I actually believe that what He does in those processes is He breaks control, He breaks manipulation, all those things and when you show up on game day with your football helmet, with the actual ear hole over here, your knees skin up, your shoulder pads on sideways and God am here to serve he says now you can rule. Then you're humble when you get there because you got there in spite of you, all of us know us and not after who people see us so we know us and when we get there and God says I brought you to have mercy on every person because I had mercy on you all the way. You are qualified because you did everything right, because you stayed with me so give that same grace to others and lift others.

About HRH Sir Clyde Rivers

King Nana Okogyeman Obremponnsu Kobina Amissah 1 (HRH Sir Clyde Rivers), The Development Chief of Ekumfi Kuotukwa, Ghana, was coronated in December 3, 2021. He is the founder of I Change Nations and a Global Civility leader.

He is the Global Board Chairman to OPAD to the United Nations – New York. Dr. Rivers has been honored internationally and has received numerous awards for excelling in his field and making a difference in people's lives.

He is the recipient of the Nelson Mandela International Peace Award 2019. HRH won the 2019 presidential Volunteer Service Award in 2017, won the United States of America Presidential life Achievement Award for over 4,000 volunteer hours serving the nation and humanity.

In 2017 HRH Rivers was given the Title of Don/Sir Dr. Rivers as he became knighted into the original Kingdom of Guatemala. In 2017 he received the Danny K. Davis Peace Prize, a U.S.A congressional Award.

Royal Mindset Like God

Royal Mindset Like God

Chapter Twelve
WHAT IS A ROYAL MINDSET?

Professor Julian Businge

I congratulate you for reading this book from introduction to the last chapter. Am glad you're among to this life changing book,

"Royal Mindset Like God", it's an honor to have a mind like Christ. You will agree with me that after finish reading this book, things will longer be the same again in your life.

A lot has been said about the royal mindset but I would like to add something to what you've learnt so far. How you see yourself how you think about yourself and this all starts with patterns in our minds.

What makes us think that way, it could be the homes where we're brought up, the schools what did they call us. Did they call you dumb? so you begin to think a certain way because all around you that's what you knew. For example, if you grew up in a home where they always said there's no money, even when you grow up and you have too much money you will always be saying there's no money because it's already in your DNA but when Jesus came He said all old things have passed away behold a new thing, the kingdom of God is here.

It is here right now, you can change your old patterns, you can change your old ways of thinking, you can change the way you see the world, how does God see you.

We are royals because that's how God sees us, that's what God calls us and so we want everybody out there to also begin to see themselves as royals accept themselves as royals. We are the children of God so if we are the seed, we are the children of God and carrying his DNA in us.

God's representative on earth so who are we? We are kings and priests, we are the chosen generation, the royal priesthood, the holy nation and we want everybody reading this book to embrace this knowledge and believe it and begin to walk in it.

So, my next question is once you know that

I'm a royal what do I need, how does it all start, what do I need to take? The first step is to begin to think differently, what do I need to do? Yes, I love the fact that I'm royal. Christ came, He died for me, you know yeah that is the first but what are some of the steps, what are some of the things? For me, I will start with what I think is the most important thing is desire to feel royal, desire it want everything starts with desire as a man thinks in his heart so he's, desire to feel and look like a royal.

In that way, your ways of thinking every time you're walking around-you're not just anybody walking around, you are somebody, so you already have that desire in you to live and feel and do everything.

1.1 That Royalty Doesn't Expire

First of all, royalty is something that does not expire, you are meant to come into this world and reign as a child of God and go back and sit in your palace that your father has prepared for you.

It doesn't expire, we are so tired of just waiting for the pie in the sky, we want to live and exercise our royal authority, our divine royalty now and here. It could start so someone is asking how can I do it. Give me the first things that I need to do, we've already said change your mindset, change the way you think and next could be giving thanks, accept that you are a royal.

Do you know what it means to accept to look at yourself in the mirror and say good morning queen, good morning king, I am a child of God, I am special, I'm a royal am born for a purpose. I am here for a divine purpose, the government of heaven is backing me, so when you begin to appreciate who you are, recognize who you are, that's a good starting point and it takes a process , it is something that you have, you know, changing old habits is not easy, it is not easy, it takes a process.

You have to be consistent and be forceful, your mind might say no you're not but say yes, I am. Sometimes you have to speak to yourself and you might even hear a voice laughing at you, you have to speak back to that voice.

When Jesus came on this earth everytime he talked of his father, I do what I see my father doing well what do we do ourselves do we do what we see our father doing absolutely because Jesus is our role model, he's our compass of how we should live a real life. They asked him so you say you were king he said so you say. I come from a kingdom, the kingdom I come from is not the same as your kingdom.

So, you have to keep reaffirming it no matter how people despise it, no matter how people may laugh at you. People may think you are going crazy but keep it up, keep going, sooner or later people will begin to even call you themselves because you yourself have accepted it, you are walking in it, you are feeling it. Everywhere you go, you touch others, you don't see them as nobodies and you appreciate them because you're all made in the same image.

You're all here for a purpose so when you meet your fellow new fellows it is something powerful, you feel the love, the power, you connect because there's no more classes, there is no middle class. You're all in the God class, the sovereign class.

Basically, this is all about you guys, it's all about walking in your royalty, in your authority, in your power. How can you discover royal genius and how can you awaken that royal power sleeping inside of you? It could be your gift, it could be an idea that has just been sleeping and needs an awakening it needs someone to recognize and appreciate and say come on it is your time, it is your season.

We are not here forever, we are in this world for a time, for a reason, for a purpose, when we go back, we must give accountability how did you do it. Jesus lived just 33 years but the impact he made we're still talking about it and that is how he wants us to live because we already have the holy spirit at work in us, we already have it, we have the breath of God, the very air that God himself breathed into us.

So, what are those limitations hindering you to walk and function? how you were created to be? So we have a free consultation feel free, anyone who feels like they are ready to work in their royalty, we have a 30 minutes consultation to see how we can help you to move forward and help you discover and develop your royal mindset but it's been an honor and a privilege.

About Professor Julian Businge

Founder of Royal Civility Global Initiative, Property, and Leadership Expert. Professor Julian Businge is a published Author, Keynote Speaker, and Business Strategist.

With practice that spans over a decade, in business with surpassed industry knowledge, her career expands over several industries, including Entrepreneurship, property, Career Growth, and Writing.

An expert in turning ideas into reality, identifying development projects and high yielding properties that generate lucrative returns. Professor Julian is a Les Brown Certified Life Coach, passionate about helping career-oriented women learn business and leadership strategies to earn financial freedom. She mentors those that wish to create long-term financial security and wealth through property investment in particular serviced Accommodation.

Additionally, Julian has had the opportunity to become a UN representative for the Peace Society of Kenya. She has published many thought-leaderships, property management articles and has been the most vital and effective in her field, and holds multiple professional designations.

A pioneer in property development, Julian is the co-founder of World Greatness Awards and Peace Apartments. She provides serviced accommodation through the platform of Airbnb.

Highlights of Julian's career include her privilege to become the Ambassador of World Civility. With the same enthusiasm, she also consistently was featured in Global Library of Female Authors, Herstory Magazine, and Iconic Influencers Magazine.

Julian earned her Doctorate Degree that significantly elevated her leadership skillset and her potential to increase credibility and opportunity. Her Degree offered her the highest lifetime earnings prospects and allowed her to pursue an unrivaled level of knowledge in her field.

She was also awarded multiple designations back to back, including Honorary Professorship in 2020, for her bestowed dedicated contribution and service. Being chosen as an Honorary Professor is a great prestige which she attained after her services with sincerity and excellence.

In the same year, in 2020, Julian Businge was honored as Great Britain Business Woman of the Year for her prolific performance.

Royal Mindset Like God

WHAT IS ROYAL CIVILITY?

It's the Biblical world view about humanity. The Culture of Royal Civility is a global initiative dedicated to helping people discover, develop, deliver and celebrate their true identity through God our Sovereign. We believe that everyone is valuable before God and has a gift that is a solution to someone else. If we truly understood who we are in Jesus and what He has done for us, everyone would be the most confident people on Earth.

Insecurity would be banished from our lives forever. We'd reign in life as kings. We'd walk around on this planet like we own it. Because, the fact is, we are divine Royalty.

We are the Royal Family of God. God is SOVEREIGNTY. We belong in the God class. Understanding the sovereignty of God is extremely important. Your value is not determined by human beings but by the one who created you. The more we know who we are, our perspectives change. Discover God's original plan for man, live every day of life completely as Royalty guaranteed of your inheritance as a child of God. Reflect every day on God's immeasurable gift!

A man's gift makes room for him, and brings him before great men. God gave you a gift to prosper in everything. If you have a special gift and you are not working to develop it, you will see it going down the drain. Gifts are very powerful; it's a man's destiny and only hope. If you ask the Holy Spirit for direction or ideas, he will give you the ideas, He will tell you what work to do so that you can prosper with your gifts but you have to work hard. This Global Initiative offers the following:

- Royal Civility publications
- Royal mind-set coaching
- Royal Fashions
- Royal Tours
- Royal Portraits
- Royal Civility institute
- Royal Civility Awards

  Royal Civility innovation and initiative is helping my community and our world by:

- During the black history month, we get into schools and youth clubs and online to talk about African Royalty and its importance to us.
- Promoting cultural exchanges between Africa and Europe
- Teaching Royal Diplomacy and protocol to the visitors from around the world or local

community ready to learn
- Travel to African Kingdoms
- Publishing books cultural and apps e.g Yega Orutooro

Find out more at:

www.royalbranding.org

www.julianbusinge.com

www.royalcivilityinsitute.com

CONCLUSION

We've come to the end of this great Book "The Mind That Rules The World." However, I would like to conclude the book by making us understand the purpose of the earth and why you are a heavenly citizen.

It's important to remind us that the Almighty God had a special purpose for creating the earth. In Isaiah 45:18, the prophet told us that, "God himself hath formed the earth and made it; he hath established it, he created it not in vain."

This means, God didn't create the earth because He had nothing doing or for nothing. He had a special purpose for creating it.

Genesis 1:1, in the beginning, God created the heaven and the earth. Now, the heaven is the spiritual realm that is inhabited by God and the heaven beings. The earth is the physical realm where plants, human being and animals inhabit. This is not enough to know the intention of God for the creation of the earth.

From a careful study of the book of Revelation, it's

clear that God's presence is in every corner of heaven. The heaven is ultimately indwelled by the presence of God and influenced by His will. Heaven is also where God has His throne. This means, God's presence and dominion is permanent in heaven.

In other words, heaven is occupied by the presence of God or the heaven is perfectly under the government of God. This means, heaven is a kingdom where God reign as the King. But don't forget that the heaven is a spiritual world.

However, God also planned to have a physical world where His presence and government would reign just as it's in heaven. God wanted a physical world where His spiritual reign would be physically made manifest.

This is the intention of God for the earth in which you and I dwell. God wanted the earth to be clothed with His presence and governed by His decrees. God want a physical world that would be a replica of heaven ruled by His will and sovereignty.

These purposes were hidden in the statement which God made when creating man. He said; let us make man in our image, after our likeness: and let them have dominion over the fish of the sea, and over the fowl of the air, and over the cattle, and over the earth, and over every creeping thing that creepeth upon the earth.

While man is to be the physical medium to establish the intention of God for the earth, the earth is intended to be under two things which are:

- The Image of God
- The Dominion of God

This means, the earth was primarily made to be ruled under God's dominion—leadership through His Image. But, for God to achieve this, He made man (You and I) who He wrapped up in His Image and empowered him through His Spirit to establish His sovereignty on the earth.

Sow This Book Into Someone's Life!

Don't let the impact of this book end with you

Contact us: royal@julianbusinge.com

Or connect on social media:

Facebook Page /Instagram: royal civility

Thank you and looking forward to celebrating with you, great testimonies, Amen.

Royal Mindset Like God

MORE OF OUR BOOKS AVAILBILE ON AMAZON

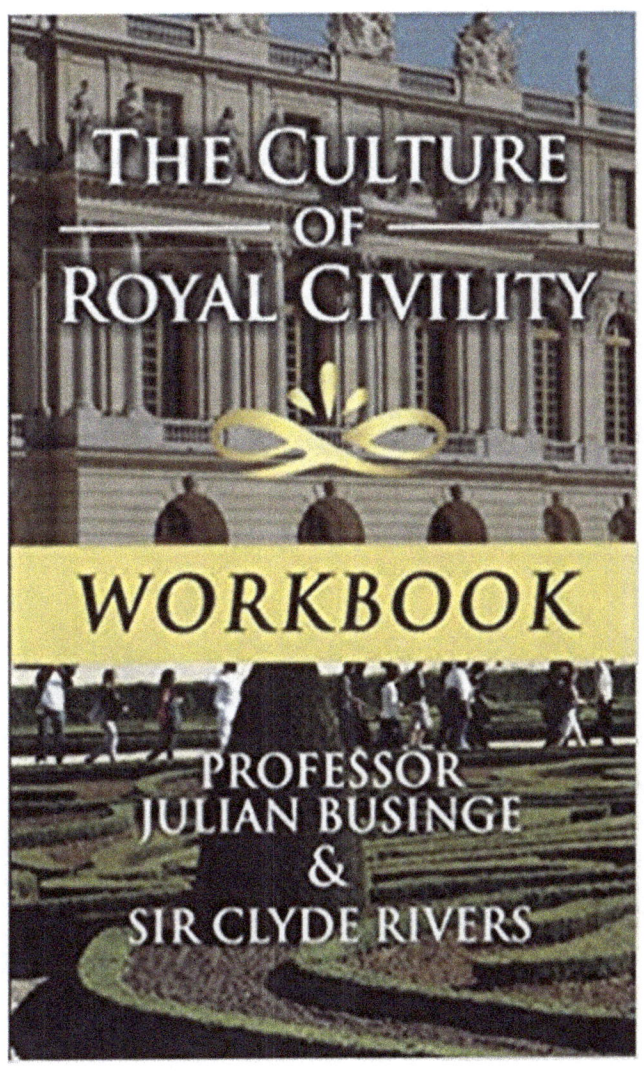

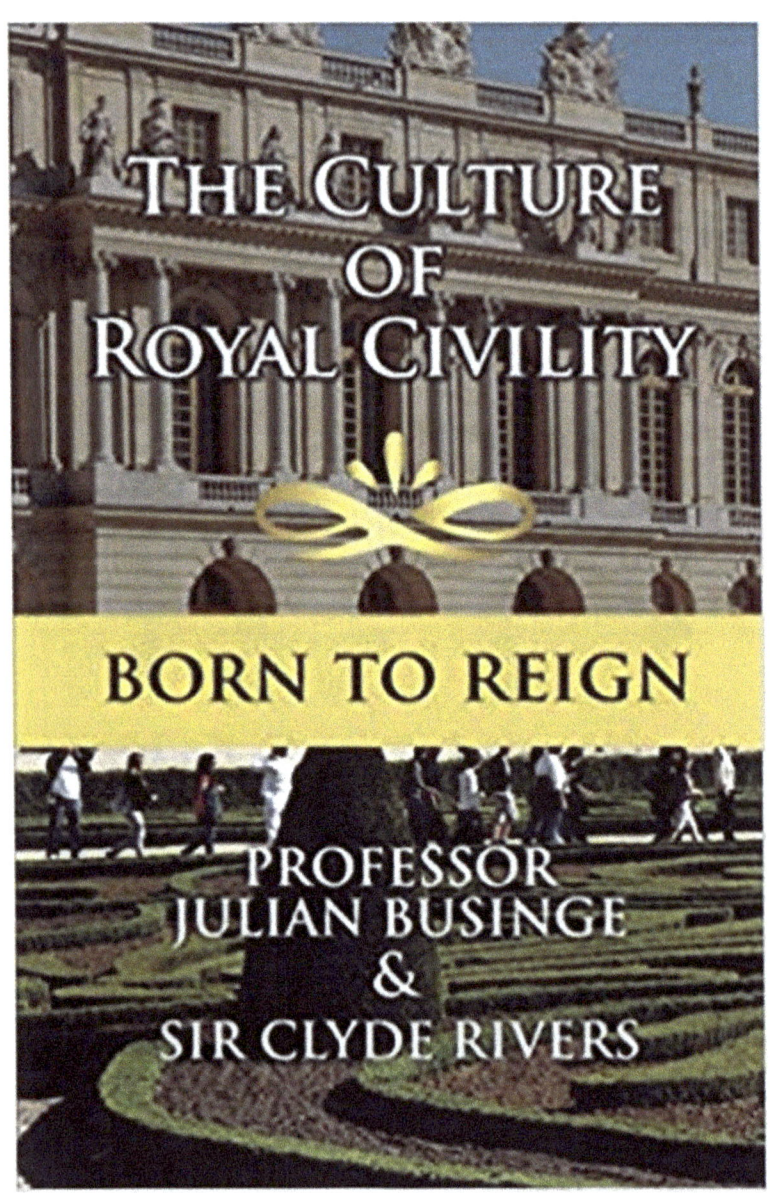

Royal Mindset Like God

Royal Mindset Like God

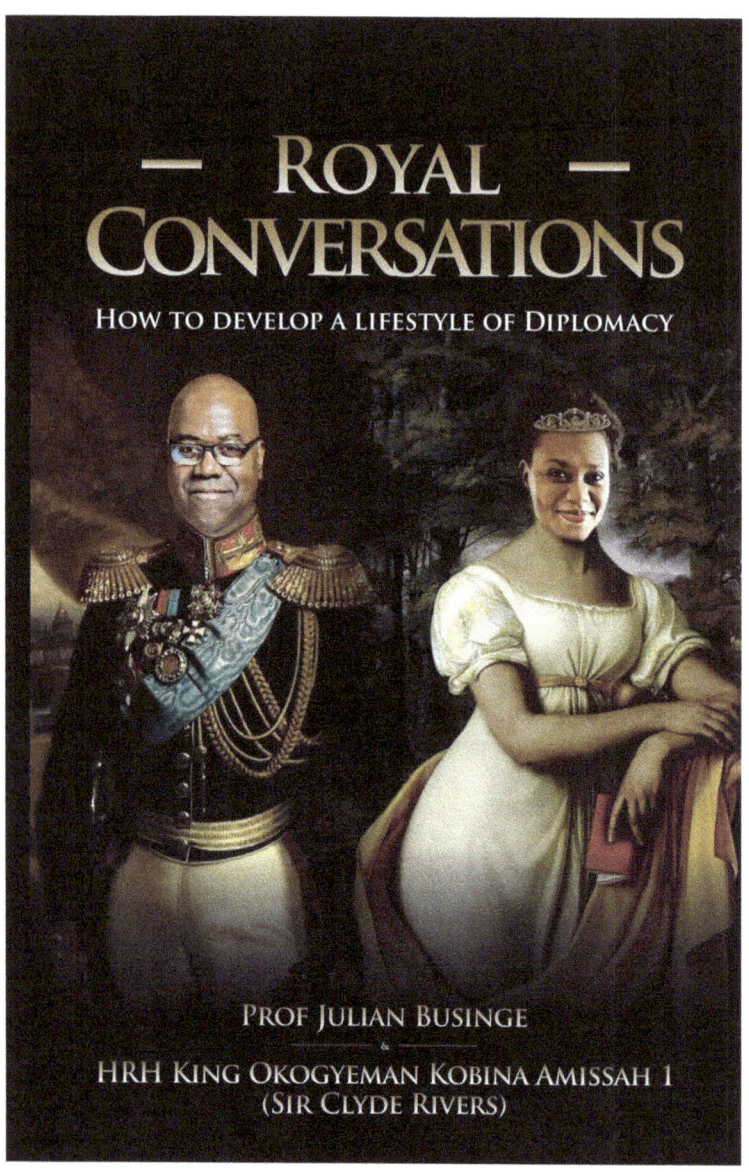

Royal Mindset Like God

www.ingramcontent.com/pod-product-compliance
Lightning Source LLC
Chambersburg PA
CBHW071216160426
43196CB00012B/2329